I0691749

Peter Charles Remondino

Longevity and climate:

Relations of climatic conditions to longevity, history, and religion: relations

of climate to national and personal habits : the climate of California and its

effects in relation to longevity

Peter Charles Remondino

Longevity and climate:
Relations of climatic conditions to longevity, history, and religion: relations of climate to national and personal habits ; the climate of California and its effects in relation to longevity

ISBN/EAN: 9783337716516

Printed in Europe, USA, Canada, Australia, Japan

Cover: Foto ©Lupo / pixelio.de

More available books at **www.hansebooks.com**

LONGEVITY AND CLIMATE.

RELATIONS OF CLIMATIC CONDITIONS TO LONGEVITY,
HISTORY AND RELIGION.—RELATIONS OF CLIMATE
TO NATIONAL AND PERSONAL HABITS.—THE
CLIMATE OF CALIFORNIA AND ITS EFFECTS
IN RELATION TO LONGEVITY.

BY

P. C. REMONDINO, M. D.

SAN DIEGO.

*(Read before the Medical Society of the State of California,
at Los Angeles, April 17, 1890.)*

WOODWARD & CO., PRINTERS, 522 CALIFORNIA ST., S. F., CAL.

LONGEVITY AND CLIMATE.

RELATIONS OF CLIMATIC CONDITIONS TO LONGEVITY, HISTORY AND RELIGION.—RELATIONS OF CLIMATE TO NATIONAL AND PERSONAL HABITS.—THE CLIMATE OF CALIFORNIA AND ITS EFFECTS IN RELATION TO LONGEVITY.

By P. C. REMONDINO, M. D., San Diego.

The art of prolonging life has made but little progress in the last hundred years. Some fifty years ago, Erasmus Wilson in editing the work of Hufeland, written over fifty years before, found but little to criticise or to add. The last work on "Old Age," by George Murray Humphry, although full of interesting and instructive material, does not add anything to what Hufeland taught a century ago. With all the progress made in physiological, chemical and hygienic science, that of prolonging life has not made a like advance. The prolongation of life, as taught by Hufeland, depends upon the strict observance of the laws of nature. It was one of his sayings, that the nearer and truer we were to Mother Earth, and the closer our intercourse with nature, the closer we approach the source of eternal youth and health; hence, it is only necessary to understand how nature intended that we should live in order to live long and comfortably, art can do nothing to assist. There are no royal roads to health or longevity, nor is there anything that money can purchase that will aid, unless it be peace, ease and contentment. There are no "elixirs of life" or fountains whose waters will grant perpetual youth. The close study of nature and her laws is all that is required; and he who can best describe the effects and applications of these laws as regards the human economy, has most advanced the science of longevity; neither the crucible of the chemist nor the dissecting knife of the anatomist nor the microscope of the physiologist can add to its knowledge. When Parr died, Harvey, who made an autopsy of the body, found that the organs were all sound and healthy and that no diseased condition existed to account for his death.

What are the conditions and circumstances that favor longevity and enable humanity to run the gauntlet of diseases and reach that old age that comes with unimpaired organs, that enables a man to live in comfort and finally pass unconsciously into that painless euthanasia that should be the natural ending of the great majority. Of these causes none has the same influence as climate, as it determines the productions of the earth and the nature of the food of which man is to partake, as well as the quality and quantity required. Besides the matter of diet which influences his inclinations and characteristics, climate in a sense exercises the determination of his choice of drink, clothing and occupation. Of these, occupation plays an important role, in determining the longevity of the individual; it defines, in a sense, the purity of the air he shall breathe, the nature of the food or drink of which he shall partake, as well as his habits and the wear and tear that he is to be subjected to. Occupation gives the average age he may be expected to live, and often determines the disease of which he is to die; besides it foretells the diseases, accidents or physical defects he may expect to encounter.

DIET.

There is probably no cause of longevity upon which opinions are as unanimous as that of diet. It is but necessary to study the lives of the early Christian Fathers to become convinced that a spare diet—even when carried to an extreme degree as to poverty of quantity and quality—is conducive to a long life. Jonas, a monk in the monastery of Mochaus, in Egypt, lived to the age of 85 years on a diet of raw herbs and sleeping on a chair. Saint Anthony and his monks ate but once a day, and this towards its close, of a little bread with salt and water for a drink, Anthony living to the age of 105. Saint Paul, the hermit, reached 115 years on a simple diet of a few dates daily. Saint Francis de Paul lived to 91, only taking a simple meal after sunset and no drink but water, besides often fasting wholly for three days in succession. The Cardinal de Salis, who died in 1785 at the age of 105, lived a very abstemious life. The effects of such a life in inducing longevity did not escape the attention of the clergy, the Jesuit Lessius observing that the fast was the greatest blessing that the Church had given to mankind, as it increased their days on earth. It was remarked by Saint Basilius that children ran less risk in their earlier years, if on a spare diet—and as physicians we well know that children who have not been on a flesh diet and living sparely are not as liable to sickness, especially enjoying a certain immunity from convulsive diseases and making a more rapid recovery when sick than children who live grossly and on flesh diet.

As to adults and old age, Sir Henry Thompson truly observes that the typical man of 80 or 90 is lean and spare and lives on a slender diet. "*Si homo parum edit et parum bibit, nullum morbum hoc inducit,*" observed Hippocrates. "Eat little and labor if you wish to be well," remarks Aristotle. Galen believed that by dieting and fasting diseases were avoided, that the delicate could be made to reach old age and that health depended upon a spare diet.

It is related of Pomponius Atticus, that, being ill of some imagined incurable ailment, he determined to starve himself to death to shorten his misery; through these means he recovered his health. Cornaro lived on twelve ounces of food and sixteen ounces of drink as his daily allowance for nearly sixty years, diminishing the quantity as age advanced; this regimen was begun at the age of forty with a broken down constitution and with no expectation of life. In the last edition of his book he thus exclaims: "Oh unhappy Italy, dost thou not see, that gluttony and excess rob thee every year of more inhabitants than pestilence, war and famine could have done." Addison mentions that Diogenes one day met a young man going to a feast, and immediately laid hold of him and carried him to his friends, as one who was running into imminent danger had he not prevented him. It was also Addison who observed that the apothecary and doctor are perpetually employed in countermining the cook and the distiller. All old people are as a rule very small eaters, and all modern writers fully agree with Cornaro, that with advancing age and diminished power of expenditure less and less food is required. To eat little, and that little of simple food, is to prolong life. "For my part," said Addison, "when I see a fashionable table set out in all its magnificence, I fancy I see gouts, and dropsies, fevers and innumerable distempers lying in ambuscade among the dishes."

The early Fathers looked upon fasting and the most simple of diets as highly conductive to chastity, which is in itself a friend to longevity; to this combination of abstemious and unstimulating diet and continence the hermits and monks of the early Christian centuries owe that extreme age that so many attained. The Egyptians interdicted the uso of fish to their priesthood as inconsistent diet for the continent and chaste. Juvenal mentions that the Romans considered oysters as an essential food for the assiduous worshipper at the shrine of Venus. The old Romans knew the value of shell-fish. On an old Celibate, this form of food would have no effect, but on a young man the stimulating properties of fish, oysters, lobsters, etc., is very apparent. The nervous excitation that often follows such a diet, was well understood by the ancients, but many of the monks, ignorant of this, imagined while abstaining from flesh and subsisting on mollusks and fish. that the arch enemy of man assailed them with all forms of carnal temptations. Being too old and unsusceptible themselves to understand the true state of affairs, the old abbots and priors laid the evident worldliness of their monks to the fattening influence of the inactive life of the cloister and to the too healthy assimilation induced by a clear conscience. The Canon of St. John was instituted to meet the requirements of these rosy cheeked and rotund monks; by it, it was ordered, that such monks as the Superior of the convent should designate, should be bled every other month, or as the Canon called it " *Monialem minuere,*" *shaving or paring* down the monk. By this process they regained that humility of countenance and demeanor, and that pallid look that was more in keeping with their calling. Origenes and his monks went even further. Fearing that, in spite of their fasts, mortifications and vigils, the devil might still succeed in his schemes of temptations, they followed the traditional habit of the castor and defied the devil afterwards. This method had at times been very successful, as, for instance, when the good old Canon Fulbert determined to make a good monk of poor old Abelard.

In the case of Origenes and his monks, it was not all smooth sailing even after this sacrifice. The Church held peculiar views, and could not connect certain reflex sensations with the diet of spiced oysters, lobster salad, or sturgeon stewed in spiced wines, but believed that the monks might sin in heart for want of proper grace, and, therefore, claimed that the continence of Origenes and his monks being now compulsory, it being entirely beyond their power to be otherwise than chaste, they had lost the main glory of a Christian, that of victoriously struggling against temptation, and by resistance, born of triumphant virtue, overcoming all the wiles of the Devil. From this view of the case the Church issued strict injunctions that no more Abelards should be manufactured, and furthermore, that none of that kind should thereafter ever be admitted to holy orders. These theological discussions do not concern us as physicians, unless it be to observe what errors in life will be committed by ignorance. A proper knowledge regarding the stimulating and other peculiar virtues and properties of foods would have saved some mutilation and much useless legislation. One point, however, suggested by the subject is of interest to us on the point of longevity: viz., that with the loss of caste and reputation they also lost their chances of longevity for which their monastic life had long prepared them.

There is not a recorded instance of a eunuch becoming a centenarian, but on the contrary, they are said to be short lived; they are, it is true, exempt from some diseases, among which Hippocrates mentions gout; but on the other hand, their tissues are lax and flabby, and they are particularly liable to visceral diseases and dropsies. Impotence, on the contrary, does not seem to shorten a man's days, or render him more liable to diseases. The diet used by many of the hermits and recluses was so unnutritious and unstimulating that impotence would be the natural result, and we must accept the temptations to which they report themselves as being subjected as being purely visionary and the result of disordered imagination resulting from long fasts and vigils; yet the ages reached by these hermits, as a class, almost staggers belief. The Turks and Arabs, who often from early indulgence, and as a result of harem life, are found impotent at the age of thirty years, seem nevertheless to reach in many cases a good old age. The Arabs are a very long lived people, and I have noticed some of the finest specimens of old age,—vigorous and active, with nothing but the white beard and hair to denote age,—among the Algerine Arabs, and from my observation, I am of the opinion that where impotence is a constant bar to incontinence, but where the physical organism is otherwise perfect, that such condition is positively favorable to longevity; this refers to men that have passed middle life before becoming so.

Dr. John Davy, quoted by Pavy, regards a fish diet as eminently tending to develop a prolific power in man. Plato regarded a fish diet as unfit for a nation who wished to maintain its independence; and the old Romans looked upon the piscivorous Rhodians with contempt. A purely fish diet is said to reduce weight without loss of bulk, and it is also considered that it produces strong muscular development. The Chinese who come to California, are mostly from the river and seaside districts of China and subsist largely on fish, yet their endurance and capacity for labor is wonderful. Among them centenarianism is considered a natural condition, as in China, according to Sir J. Bowring, the age of from ninety to one hundred forms the tenth division of the life of man, or as they term it "Age's extremity." In connection with this subject of fish diet, chastity and longevity, Hecquet relates that the Sultan Saladin, wishing to know the relative merits of a flesh diet or one of fish on the chastity of man, subjected a number of dervishes to restricted diet of flesh, subjecting them in the meantime to continued temptations; they were afterwards fed exclusively on fish with a continuance of the temptations. It is related that they stood out without any great effort while subsisting on meat, but after a few days of fish diet they easily fell from grace.

From the above it is evident that a knowledge of medicine and its collateral sciences is paramount to all else. The true student of his art does not confine his research to the action of castor oil or rhubarb; he must cull his knowledge from all sources, for everything that may affect health or life belongs to his domain. The most noted physicians of every age have been those noted for their close observance of facts, and defiance of all conventionalities that interfered with the pursuit of knowledge and the exercise of their convictions. Human nature and its peculiarities have much to do with shortening or lengthening life. The effects of vice are, as a rule, detrimental, except that of avarice, which through its abstemiousness of diet and provision for the future, and the ease of body and mind which it produces, is conceded to be very favorable to a long life. All the old historical misers have reached old age.

In addition to the benefits to be derived from fasts, longevity is further indebted to the Holy Church for its Canons with regard to continence. Dachèry tells us, that the Canons of Ireland prescribed continence to the married at the following periods, to wit: during the three lenten seasons, before Easter, St. Johns and Christmas, of forty days each; then for all Sundays, Wednesdays and Fridays, throughout the year, and during the period of gestation; and after delivery, for forty-six days in case the child was a girl and for thirty-six days if a boy. On the Continent where it was found that the Laity adhered more to the letter than to the spirit of the Canons, it was found necessary by the Bishop of Noyon, to include concubines in his prescriptions for the periods of continence.

The pious Wasselin, Abbe of Liege, counseled prayer as beneficial before the act, which would prevent a too free indulgence.

We are now prepared to understand how St. Louis, who was an enthusiast in religious matters, as well as in their strict observance, should have had his own particular calendar of fasts and continences, and that the latter should be a very rigorous one; it included all the lents, advents, feasts and other solemnities, periods which in those days absorbed every day in the year, all of which practice was perfectly consistent with the pious and religious habits of the time. The Queen Eleanor was from the Atlantic shores of Southern France, whose warm soil and gentle sea breezes, combined with the stimulating diet of the country, tend rather to develop a Cleopatra than a nun. She was young, impassioned and handsome, and historians agree without mentioning what share the King's calendar had in the matter, "that she was also much dissatisfied at the scrupulous and superstitious attentions which he paid to his devotions." It ended in a rupture and we finally find the fair but frail Eleanor divorced from her calendared saint and married to Henry II of England, a tall, majestic, strong-limbed and broad-chested Norman—the father of the future Richard, the Lion-hearted, but what was more to the point—a king who had lost his calendar.

Incredible as it may sound, this strict observance of the precepts of virtue and adherence to the restrictions of his calendar by St. Louis were the means of plunging England and France into a long succession of wars.

It happened that with her marriage to Henry, Eleanor carried to the English Crown her heritage of a portion of France. From this arose those endless wars that made Edward the Black Prince and Crecy, and to which the Prince of Wales owes the three-plumed crests on his coat of arms. Neither Henry the Fifth and the Field of Azincourt nor the Maid of Orleans, nor the lamented and romantic Rosamond Clifford, the fair Rosamond of Woodstock, would have occupied such a place in history but for the saintly Louis and his unpracticable calendar. Any intelligent medical man could have foreseen all this and prevented it, but it just happens that where medical counsel is most required it is just most neglected. A Hammond or a Brown-Sequard would simply have filled the gay and festive Eleanor with bromide of sodium and potassium, and the sad and pensive Louis with some phosphorated Damiana tonics, lobster salad and a few spiced oysters washed down with generous draughts of champagne; this would have brought about an amicable understanding and averted all calamities. The first duty of a statesman is evidently to study medicine. Had the sage and good Suger, the prime minister of Louis the Seventh, been less an abbot or ecclesiastic and more of a physician, and been capable of seeing things from a worldly standpoint and reason things from a physical basis, like a Draper, a Heckel or a Buckle, what bloodshed and what misery would have been averted to France! Medicine may well be termed the first and basic science of all sciences. Wellington, the victor of many hard fought battles in India, Portugal and Spain, and the winner of Waterloo, was finally vanquished by a meal of hashed venison. Yet he had carefully examined the field of Waterloo and determined on its many advantages as a defensive battlefield long before Napoleon sailed with his 400 from the Island of Elba; but he had never devoted a moment's time to studying the immediate danger that might arise from an overloaded stomach—the lines of Torres Vedras and the highway from Quatre-Bras to Brussels he could defend, but the simple highway to his stomach was beyond his comprehension.

Men do not use the same general good sense in the consideration of diet in regard to their own species that they do in regard to the domestic animals entrusted to their charge. The horseman knows better than to give grain to the colt; he realizes that a colt on spare diet will make a better and more enduring horse. The dog fancier does not allow his young whelps to have meat, and as they grow up their diet is carefully watched as to quality and quantity. The trainer of the athlete does not allow his pupil, when training for the ring, the foot or boat race, to eat indiscriminately; the diet is here recognized as a great factor in making or unmaking the physique, in hardening the tissues to greater endurance and making him supple and active; to this end his diet is regulated to a fraction, strong drink is interdicted, and the continence to which were subjected the athletes of ancient Rome and Greece is here temporarily enforced. As strange as it may seem, the knowledge possessed by these trainers has been handed down by tradition, much of their art coming down through the mists of time from the old Greek and Roman temples or gladiatorial arenas by word of mouth. Why should not the benefit of the knowledge that gives a dog, a horse or an athlete a good and lasting constitution be likewise used to benefit the human race at large. In New York we have children asylums where meat diet is interdicted for the first five years of life; it is a matter worthy of remark that the children of these institutions enjoy better health and recover more promptly when sick than meat-fed children. It is well known that children still at the breast escape diseases and epidemics that often prove fatal to children on a mixed diet. I have observed this in diphtheria and other diseases. That this practice of promiscuous dieting and overfeeding children prematurely ages many, I am certain, and it is certain to be detrimental to the prospects of longevity. The evil effects of an inappropriate diet is nowhere better to be seen than in the sickly and stunted young of the dog or the colt that have had too much meat or grain. The damage done to these animals is lasting. From this it is natural and reasonable to believe that much of the moral, mental and physical stunting and subsequent bodily ill-health in the human family arises from the carelessness and indulgence of childhood. No menagerie keeper, however ignorant, would for a moment allow his inactive beasts to be fed as some of our otherwise sensible men feed themselves; the result is but too well known to them. How an intelligent human being will deliberately, of his own free will and accord, put himself in the position of a Strasburger goose, as is daily done by thousands, is a mystery past comprehension, and he has no reason to be surprised when called out of this world before his days are naturally half gone.

A happy contented disposition and a small desire for food greatly depend upon the condition of the climate. The fasts and lents submitted to with cheerfulness in the milder climates of Italy, France or Spain, or the more pronounced abstinence indulged in by the hermits of Northern Africa or the Orient, could not be well borne in the more rigorous and trying climates of Northern countries; hence we find some centuries ago low mutterings to be heard and rebellion brewing in the German convents; it was interpreted that beer was not included as an article to be abstained from in fasting or in lent, an interpretation that ended in the making of lent a season of carousal and beer. How much this may have done in developing in the monkish minds the ideas that subsequently led to the Reformation may well be a matter of conjecture.

It is related by Sir Thomas Browne that in the wars waged by Rome in the Orient, the bodies of the Roman dead underwent speedy decomposition and decay, while the corpses of the slain Persians remained dry and uncorrupted. The Persians and Syrians were an extremely abstemious people, a little flour and a few herbs being sufficient for their sustenance. Xenophon tells us that King Cyrus had accustomed his people to living on only one meal a day. These people were then, as they are now, a very long lived nation, and from Browne's remarks, their tissues, from want of grossness, must have carried their tenacity and resistance even unto death, as evidenced by the different results among the dead after a battle. The German monks after death, if placed alongside of one of the abstemious dead monks of the East, would probably have shown a greater difference than that existing between the corpses of the dead Romans and Persians as to the corruptibility; the one being meat and beer fed, and the tissues containing all the elements of fermentation and putrefaction, whilst the other by long and rigid abstinence had prepared his body throughout life for the process of speedy and natural mummification. The effects of such different conditions on the duration of life are self-evident. Still, this is not a matter of race or nationality, but the result of climatic influences; place a German monk in the seclusion of the desert wilderness and mild climate of Asia Minor, and after a few years, he will adapt himself to the Saracenic simplicity of diet, and in the end become as abstemious in life, and at death make as respectable a natural mummy as any Oriental hermit. It must likewise be admitted, that if the Oriental monk or hermit were transported to rigorous Northern Germany, he would find in the climate a positive hindrance to the continuation of his austere and abstemious habits. It is not then astonishing that in the 9th century, owing to the ignorance of the clergy in regard to physical laws, we should find the Greek monks reproaching their Gaulish brethren with their voracity. This caused Sulpicius Severus to observe, that what was in Greece considered excess at the table, was in Gaul by its climate rendered into a positive necessity. This difference in religion and its influences as well as results, is now understood. During the Franco-Prussian War when it was suggested to Bismarck, that if the Pope were driven out of Italy he might find an asylum and install himself in Northern Germany, he observed that the influence of the Pope in the climate of Germany and the influence of the Pope in the climate of Italy were two entirely different affairs, and he had no dread that the Holy Father could ever make any trouble in the Fatherland. The climate of Germany is not conducive to saintliness of the Vatican order.

Spare diet if conducive to longevity is not by any means inimical to endurance or bold deeds; nor is a climate by its great equability and mildness emasculating. This has been sufficiently proven by the daring and successful wars of the Saracenic conquests; by the fierceness of their prosecution and dash in all Moslem warlike enterprises by the Arabians, and the great endurance under privation, exposure and exertion borne by the Saracenic soldiers or the African soldiery of Hannibal under skies less genial than their own. But for the outnumbering hosts of the heavy armed and armoured men that all Europe marshalled against the Saracen on the field of Poitiers;—the date and herb-fed son of the desert, raised under a mild and cloudless blue sky to the immartial life of a simple shepherd would have made of all Europe a Caliphate.

There is one very important point in relation of diet to longevity that must not be overlooked, to wit: that all natures and dispositions are not alike. We are not all like Pomponius Atticus, already mentioned, who recovered from some incurable disease while trying to starve himself to death, nor are we like Cornaro, who, when on the brink of the grave, not only recovered from his malady by rigid abstinence, but actually managed to live to nearly a hundred years. Neither would our capture by Barbary pirates and the meagre diet and compulsory labor at the oar of an Algerine Corsair, have such a fortunate ending as that of the rich and gouty old priest mentioned by Fothergill in his work on Gout, who, by such a fortune or misfortune, was happily cured of his gout. Many a poor fellow after a few weeks of the galley bench has only been unchained that his corpse might be cast into the sea. The known asthenic condition of the many ailments requiring supporting treatment and diet are so numerous, that in them to seek health by abstinence would be but to court speedy death. I have known former *bon-vivants*, who by ill-advised counsel changed their mode of life to a spare and frugal diet, owing to kidney, liver or some other organic disease, who soon paid for the mistake with their lives. A friend, having accidentally read a copy of Cornaro, resolved with great determination to change his mode of life and, like Cornaro, become a centenarian; four months were sufficient, and the wild waves of Lake Michigan now beat the shore in sight of a beautifully moulded grassy mound that covers his remains. All the cases that have reached old age through a life of continued feasting and stuffing, proved that they had a wonderful power of resistance and of endurance; but it must also be admitted that in their case abstemiousness would, in many instances, have proved anything but a step to longevity. There is a happy medium in all things, and a discriminating knowledge is required in these matters to determine the line of demarkation between those that belong to the rule and those that belong to the exception. A mistaken or ill-advised counsel may mean death to the patient. Boerhaave once was called to a patient, who had been taken ill during his absence, and whom he found on the verge of the grave, owing to the strict diet and debilitating drinks that had been prescribed by the attending physician; generous wines and nutritious soups were at once prescribed by Boerhaave, and the patient was restored to health. Sydenham once cured a patient who had long been ill, and was supposed to be at the point of death, by stopping all medicine and removing all restrictions, substituting roast fowl and a bottle of Canary wine. Dio Lewis looked on a sensitive stomach as the rampart of health and long life. Fontenelle on the other hand, looked upon a good and vigorous stomach as one of the main requisites of long life, himself being possessed with a remarkably good stomach, which he indiscriminately filled with all manner of good things, anchovies fried brown in olive oil being one of his favorite dishes; Fontenelle became a centenarian.

WINES AND LIQUORS,

Used unnecessarily or to excess, are a frightful source of disease, early decay and death. Garrod believed that if fermented liquors had never been indulged in, it would be questionable if gout would have ever existed. The production and use of alcoholic liquors are also influenced by climate, and the question of repressing their abuse has been variously treated, unfortunately too often in a spirit of ignorance, which carried with it neither conviction nor good results. The State Board of Health of Massachusetts has adopted the most intelligent plan towards the solution of the subject of "how shall we rid the land of intemperance;" it treats the subject as it would a disease, looking to the physical laws that govern its production and into the cosmic laws that influence its spread and propagation.

Henry I. Bowditch, the Chairman of the Committee that had this subject in hand, in his report, published in the volume of 1872, after a careful review of reports from every nation and climate, comes to the conclusion, "that a tendency to inordinate indulgence and intoxication, seems to vary with varying climatic laws and that the prevalence of intemperance over the entire globe is under the influence of a great cosmic law which confines it within certain isothermal lines. In a country like the United States, being as it is in the temperate region, the people, more or less imbued with one habit, fashion and custom, do to a certain extent override the effects of the above law, or will at least for a time; but any one who travels in California now, who visited the country prior to the general vine-planting and wine-making, will be struck with the lessening amount of the use of intoxicants and intemperance that now prevails in the State. The climatic law is here beginning to override fashions by the introduction of the juice of the grape. The cause is natural; California has a bracing exhilarating climate; this was well observed by Blodget in his work on our Climatology. Dr. Tyler of the McLean Asylum for the Insane, in the third annual Massachusetts Board of Health Reports, observes that the climate of England when compared to that of the New England Coast, is found to be depressing; and that on our Western Coast the climate is especially exhilarating. A person laboring under a depression in New England will recover by going to California. The south of Europe has a like exhilarating effect. Dr. Tyler says further that from the frequency of his observations, he is satisfied that the change in feelings, are due to the effects of climate and not to a mere change of place or scene. This stimulating effect of the California climate removes the desire and necessity for strong drinks, and the light wines of the country, by replacing the stronger liquors, will, in time, so operate, that intemperance will here be as rare as it is in Southern Europe, where, to use the classic language of John Bell, "the populace of the cities and the inhabitants of the country will be found quaffing their cool lemonade or merely cool water, slightly acidulated with lemon juice, with a *gusto* at the time, and a freshness of feeling and a hilarity of expression afterwards which neither Tokay nor Champagne, still less Madeira or Port, could supply to their votaries."

Bowditch notes that the same amount of liquor that is well borne in England with its depressing climate, will, if persisted in for the same length of time in New England, develop into delirium tremens, and that persons who cannot use liquor in New England, can easily do so in the English climate. California offers a still greater bar to the use of intoxicants than New England, owing to its more exhilarating climate. This cannot make of California but a land of enforced temperance resulting from climatic laws and also by the same means a land of greater longevity.

It is interesting and edifying to notice the misdirected wisdom and want of great foresight with which legislation has dealt with the subject of liquor, and the injurious and unhappy results that have followed its enactments. In England during the middle of the 17th century, while that interminable war with France was in one of its peculiarly eruptive periods, the Government began to meddle with the importation of light French wines, which had been used since the Roman conquest, and that up to that date were as much of a family drink and an article of food, with the English people, as it is to-day with the French. As observed by Gladstone, even the University of Oxford, foreseeing the evil that would follow these restrictions and the inevitable habit of using stronger drink, that would take the place of the excluded light wines, petitioned Parliament against the heavy duties which it was about to lay on French wines. Parliament, however, in its ignorance, only saw the injury they were inflicting upon the French; they could not be made to see the evil result that it would have upon England. As remarked by Macaulay, the displacement of the light wines brought about the use of punch, rum and gin. Families formerly accustomed to their light wine at meals or as a part of their home hospitality, were compelled to resort to the stronger liquors, and the effect was plainly visible over the land; notably in the increase of crime. By the year 1703 and with the conclusion of the treaty of Methuen, when the light wines of France were practically excluded, and the English acquired the habit and taste for the heavy wines of Portugal, the use of light wines almost entirely disappeared from England, and port wine became now the recognized national drink and dinner beverage. These restrictions were not removed until 1831, and the taste for light wines could not now replace the habits and tastes that had been growing on the nation for several generations. How much harm this has been to England, how much gout, rheumatism, liver and kidney diseases with their apoplectic seizures and other terminations, and how much immorality and crime all this produced, can only be conjectured. English people have their former ministry and their Parliament to thank for all these ills and physical and moral disturbances.

The United States have come in for their share of all the evils entailed by the action of the thick-headed ministry of Queen Anne. England was the parent country, and its habits crossed the Atlantic along with the blunderbuss and broad brimmed hats of the period. Our heterogeneous population, the German and his beer, the Frenchman and his wine, the Dutchman with his gin, the New Englander with his rum, and the intrusive and infectious festive disposition of the light hearted Celt and Gael which pervaded the land and even now rules politics, have formed for the American Nation habits, partly results of heredity, acquired tastes and fashions that will be hard to eradicate, but that tell on the morality, health, comfort and longevity of its people. The American Government, in imitation of the British Ministry of 1703, has foolishly done everything towards obstructing the importation of light French wines by the imposition of heavy duties, thus placing these wines only within the reach of the very wealthy, thereby encouraging the taste and forming the habit of drinking whisky, a national taste and habit which to the inhabitants of Southern Europe is something incomprehensible. The harm done by the Government was inevitable, as no light wines were then made in the country; but now that California bids fair to exceed the vintage of France, we have at hand the only solution of the temperance question that is practicable.

Old men, and even very old men, are often cited as examples of the harmless nature of strong drink; as remarked by Matthews, some of the toughest constitutions, resembling lignum vitæ in their textures, have been possessed by persons who are hardly ever sober except when they are drunk. Daniel Bull McCarthy of Kerry, Ireland, who drank freely of undiluted rum and brandy during the last seven years of his life, died in 1752 at the age of 111; George Kirton, of Oxnop Hall, Yorkshire, who died in 1764 at the age of 120, was also a hard drinker; William Hearst, a farm laborer of Micklefield, Yorkshire, who died very old in 1853, considered rum the balm of his life, and spent for it all the money he received from the parish. These examples only prove that there are exceptions to the rule; but the preponderance of testimony is in favor of sobriety and temperance. Very aged persons who have used tobacco all their lives are often pointed out as examples of its harmlessness, but the profession are too well acquainted with its effects not to know that tobacco is a very potent factor in making life shorter. The late M. Chevreul who reached the age of 103, did not use tobacco, nor did M. Renandin, another French centenarian who passed his 105 years. All exceptions to the harmfulness of alcohol or tobacco are in keeping with the remarkable case of Lady Lewson, who reached the age of 106 years, and attributed her great old age to the fact that she never washed.

TEMPERATURE.

A fall of temperature or any sudden meteorological change is very prejudicial to the aged, and in the temperate regions variability of temperature presents a formidable barrier to our efforts to reach old age. Cold especially has a very deleterious influence on the aged. We are told that King David, when in his old age, was kept alive by the animal heat imparted to his wasted body by sleeping with a young Sunamite maid; and as it was by similar performances that King David had lost his vitality, this is undoubtedly the first recorded instance of the practice of homeopathy. Boerhaave also adopted a like practice to restore the ebbing vitality of an old Dutch Burgomaster; but as the Netherlands are more humid and cold than Palestine, and from the natural frigidity that soil and climate imparts to the inhabitants, it took two Dutch maidens, simultaneously employed, to accomplish in Boerhaave's case what a single Sunamite maid did for King David. The Romans, when old and infirm, if financially able, removed to Naples or to some of the neighboring islands or sea shores, to reside during the winter season, on account of the reputed influence of the milder climate in promoting longevity. Hufeland states that "uniformity in the state of the atmosphere, particularly in regard to heat, cold, gravity and lightness, contributes in a very considerable degree to the duration of life. Countries, therefore, where great and sudden variations in the barometer and the thermometer are usual cannot be favorable to longevity. Such countries may be healthy and men may become old in them, but they will not attain to a great age, for all rapid variations are so many internal revolutions; and these occasion an astonishing consumption both of the powers and the organs." According to his observations, islands and peninsulas have been at all times the cradles of old age. "In islands mankind always becomes older than in continents lying under the same degree of latitude, thus men live longer in the islands of the Archipelago than in the neighboring countries of Asia; in Cyprus than in Syria; in Formosa and Japan than in China; and in England and in Denmark than in Germany. Salt water also is more favorable to longevity than fresh, and for that reason seafaring people become so old. A great deal seems to depend likewise on the ground and soil; and in this respect a cold soil seems to be the least calculated to promote longevity." It is also remarked by Hufeland, that Switzerland, owing to its variable weather, produced fewer cases of longevity than Scotland. Tissot of Lausanne speaks of the poor ventilation of the Swiss houses and counsels the sick man rather to be carried to his barn, where the air is purer from free ventilation, than to die miserably in his warm but unventilated house. The great and sudden changes of temperature in the Swiss Alps, and the extreme ranges of heat and cold, make it an undesirable and unfavorable climate for the aged; the rigors of the climate and the at times very low temperature make perfect ventilation next to impossible. Life, under such circumstances, has to run too many gauntlets successfully to reach old age.

Day in his diseases of old age, observing the reduced heating power of the aged, mentions the case of a man 121 years of age, who came to Paris from Mount Jura to pay his respects to the National Assembly in the time of the French Revolution, who even in the dog days shivered with cold if not near a good fire. According to a table prepared by Quetelet with 400,000 cases as a basis, Day found that twice as many people past the age of sixty years died in December as in the warm month of July, and that the cold months of December, January, February and March combined, give nearly one-half of the deaths that happen for the whole year. Hufeland regarded either extreme of temperature as dangerous, and counseled a cool rather than a warm or hot medium as the most compatible to old age, looking upon a temperature within doors of 66 F., as the most desirable. Artificially overheated rooms he termed dangerous. Good ventilation and a certain amount of out-of-door bodily exercise he considered of the greatest importance and of the greatest necessity in ensuring good, refreshing sleep as well as a good old age.

All climatic conditions that are favorable to a long life are to be found in the most favored of marine climates where great and sudden changes are impossible and extremes of temperature are unknown. It has been imagined that southerly and mild climates must necessarily be enervating and debilitating and cannot develop a strong race; that such races must lack vigor and endurance. Yet the Saracens already mentioned indicate a powerful degree of hardiness, vigor and endurance and other facts go to show that mild climates are favorable towards developing a race of superior vitality and endurance. From the experience derived from the Russian campaign of 1812, Baron Larrey furnished many convincing proofs of the greater vitality of races born and developed in the milder climates of Europe, even when exposed to the hardships and rigors of unused to and rigorous climates. Dr. Mestivier, long a resident of Moscow, and General de Baume, who, by being with the army of Prince Eugene, which was composed mainly of his Italian subjects, had ample opportunities for more particular observation, both agree with Baron Larrey that the southern troops resisted the effects of hardships, privations and cold better than those from the north. One instance mentioned by Larrey in this regard is worth repeating. Of the third regiment of grenadiers of the guard composed of Hollanders, numbering 1787 officers and privates, only 42 returned to France, while the other two regiments of grenadiers consisting of men who were, with few exceptions, from the southern provinces of France, preserved a pretty large part of their soldiers. The loss among the German contingent was also much greater than that of the French. Larrey makes particular mention that of the Grand Army, composed as it was from troops from all of

Western Europe, the French, Portuguese, Spaniards and Italians were those from whose ranks was derived the smallest number of victims.

The endurance developed in the animal body by the California climate is wonderful. It is only of late years that this gift of climate has received recognition. The endurance of the early natives was proverbial, and the hardiness and endurance of the descendants of the soldiery that accompanied the early missionaries to this coast has always been commented upon. With little food there are few that can stand equal with the Native Californian. He is a born horseman and the feats of horsemanship that the California born *vaquero* will perform and his insensibility to fatigue are astonishing; not only has he endurance but courage, agility and strength in a surprising degree. The native horse must needs go to Arabia for his equal, either in speed, endurance, strength or intelligence. Nor are these characteristics, as commonly supposed, purely racial, for since the establishment of stables of thoroughbreds on the Pacific slopes, with the progeny of these purely bred horses has come the discovery that the wonderful and much desired peculiarities of the California native breed was purely the result of climate. The Eastern horse has been found to improve in size, compactness of muscle, wind, strength of limb and power of endurance. The records made by native born California thoroughbreds on Eastern race courses, and the wonderful developments seen in the two and three years olds on the California breeding farms have furnished all the required evidence. Senator Stanford's stables furnish some of the finest examples of these results of the influence of the California climate on the animal economy as exhibited in the horse. Not alone is the breed improved by being born here, but what is more remarkable, an Eastern horse is improved in all the qualities so much admired by horsemen by one or more seasons passed on the coast, a result that has been tested more than once; and although there is no climate the horse can put forth all its energies to so great an advantage as that of California, the increased vitality and endurance that has been generated even by one season in this atmosphere, will made itself evident long after the return of the horse from the East.

These climatic effects are not by any means restricted to the horse. Man experiences the same benefits in as full a degree and he and his progeny are as greatly benefited. The new comer from a high altitude certainly experiences some strange sensations—something that he would notice at any other point at sea level; but these are merely the results of a sudden change of atmospheric pressure and soon pass away, leaving him younger in feeling and with increased power of all the functions of life. Both men and women are alike improved and rejuvenated, the only disagreeable occurrence that may result from this being the possible advent of a late and unlooked-for Benjamin to people advanced in years,—evidence that the hands on the dial plate of time may be set back for a decade or more.

Where can a region be found where such combinations exist as described by Hufeland, where the latitude gives warmth and the sea or ocean the tempering winds; where the soil is warm and dry and the sun also bright and warm; where uninterrupted clear weather and a moderate temperature are the rule; where neither extremes of heat or cold are to be found; where free and constant ventilation is a possibility; where nothing may interfere with the daily exercise of the aged; and where the actual results and cases of longevity will bear testimony as to the efficacy of all its climatic conditions being favorable to a long and comfortable existence; or in the words of the late Professor S. D. Gross, " Where is the paradise on earth, where man may reach his three scores and ten, as promised, and do so without pain or suffering ? " The Biblical Eden must have presented just such a climatic condition as is now found in the southern part of California: limpid water for drink and delicious fruits for food, with cloudless skies, where in bright sunshine and balmy breezes life glides on from day to day in one season of everlasting spring. Europe has no such climate, nor is it to be found elsewhere in America outside of the southern shores of California. In those remote times it was called the Garden of Paradise, and now its California counterpart can with truth and justice be called the paradise of the world.

MARINE AIR.

Popular errors as to causes are very deep-rooted and persistent and sometimes become traditionally sacred and enshrined even in the tabernacle of the profession. The effects of altitude, harsh climate, variability, and extreme dryness of the atmosphere in prolonging life have been terribly exaggerated, while those of sea-level, mild climate, equability and moderate moisture have for some reason never received the attention to which they are entitled. Lombard of Geneva, in his early writings, demonstrated that occupations associated with more or less humidity were the reverse of unhealthy, basing his opinion on a series of observations made in Paris and Geneva, and from a careful consideration of the hospital records of France, Germany, Switzerland and Italy. Thachrah, who wrote on Trades in relation to Health at about the same period, came to a similar conclusion from his English observations. As to the effect on man of a marine air, Fonssangrives and Martinenq of the French Navy, Boudin and Wilson, of England, and Medical Inspectors Turner and Gihon of our own navy, all agree, as a result of their collected investigations, that marine climates give an immunity from phthisis, not enjoyed by either continental or mountainous regions. The vital statistical reports of the national navies, and what is more surprising, even those of the merchant marine of England, where men are made to live in flagrant defiance of all moral and hygienic laws, all go to support their conclusions. According to Haviland, an authority often quoted by Richardson, such a climate as that possessed by California, must, from the free access of sea air, possess an immunity from heart and kindred diseases, and the character of the soil must give to its inhabitants a like immunity from cancer.

Moist marine air and equable temperature produce the most perfect specimens of physical development. It seems a difficult matter for many to realize that atmospheric moisture derived from the ocean or great lakes, is in itself, not only harmless, but highly beneficial to health and conducive to longevity—unlike soil moisture laden with filth ferments, disease germs, and all manner of miasma.

Thus, marine nations have less consumption, less pulmonary and heart diseases, less abdominal diseases, are hardier and live longer than others; they are less despondent and less subject to nostalgia or suicide; and the more pronounced the sea influences the more pronounced are these exemptions and conditions. California has without an exception, considering the extent of its coast, the driest and warmest soil that is to be found in any practicably habitable portion of the globe. It has the hardiest, longest living and healthiest population imaginable, and an atmospheric moisture that entitles it to be classed as a climate of high humidity,—a combination of very rare occurrence;—the mean relative humidity in July being at San Diego ten per cent greater than that of St. Paul, Minn., or of Bismarck, Dakota, for the same month. Our humidity is, however, all from the sea; the soil and vegetation even greedily taking instead of imparting moisture from the air. There is in California, as a rule, no soil moisture; it is this that accounts for the utter absence of malaria near to the ocean; the atmosphere is one of considerable humidity which gradually lessens as the sea is distanced and the mountain crests approached. This is one of the great secrets of the healthfulness and longevity that is observed and enjoyed in California, and that makes of the State an incomparable hygienic Utopia. Sea level and marine air produce the sailor, who constantly lives in an air of maximum pressure and of maximum moisture; and yet, who is tougher, hardier, more enduring, lighter hearted, and longer lived than the proverbially jolly old Jack Tar?

CLIMATE AND PERSONAL BEAUTY.

One feature noted by A. N. Bell as peculiar to localities of mild climates is the personal beauty of its inhabitants. This remarkable result of climatic conditions has been the theme of praise by all the early explorers whose ships anchored in our placid waters. The finely developed and handsome appearance of the women of this coast and of the neighboring islands to the westward, aroused the admiration of even the early missionaries. The impression made by these dusky maids on the ancient mariners as they floated about the calm waters of our bays in their light boats, must have been something akin to that made by Cleopatra, as she was being rowed up the Cydnus, on the heretofore unsusceptible Anthony.

Helen, whose beauty convulsed Greece, and but for whom Homer would have had no theme, and Lais, the fair Corinthian, were both developed in a marine atmosphere. Aspasia, whose beauty and intelligence for a time ruled the destinies of Greece, was, like Venus, born from the wave. The sculptor Scopas found his ideal Venus in the Island of Egina and the modern sculptor Canova found his ideal of the goddess in the Island of Corsica. Phryne, whose beauty disarmed her judges, was, as it were, born of the sea. Where but under a genial sun and on warm soil fanned by the soft sea air could a Cleopatra have been developed or a Zenobia have been produced?

Personal beauty and longevity are akin to each other and may be said to go hand in hand. The unwrinkled countenance, clear complexion and bright eye, firm contour of limb and body and an active, soft, smooth and healthy skin, with soft hair, are as essential to attain and enjoy old age as they are to the perfection of beauty. Professional beauties are proverbially long-lived. The famous beauty, Madame Recamier, lived to a very old age. Ninon de Lenclos, who was, in her time, what the fair Lais was to ancient Greece, also lived and retained her beauty to a great age, and wherever personal beauty is carried past middle age, a long life can as a rule be predicted. Even that old Jezebel, whose beauty of form, mental accomplishments and excess of animal spirits were joined to the too great continence and sanctity of Louis VII, which embroiled Europe in so much strife and blood, lived to the age of 81.

Those beautiful sirens, whose kiss lured the mariner into oblivion, and those fabled mermaids full of beauty and grace, were no doubt suggested to the inspired poet or artist by the exceeding loveliness and beauty, as well as by the superior accomplishments and gentleness of heart and soul that pervades the maidenhood of islands and sea shores. Columbus and the early discoverers were lost in admiration of the beautiful forms of the maids of the West Indies, whose lithe and supple and shapely forms, full of health and vigor, were a surprise to these Spaniards, accustomed to muscular maids of the Dulcinea del Toboso standard of beauty. That this wonderful beauty and grace were purely the result of climatic effect is evident, as these same islands have given a like personal characteristic to the Europeans who have since peopled them. The females of the Islands of the Pacific have likewise been celebrated for the beauty of their form. The Britons whose descendants and successors receive from their island home the gift of a strong constitution, great vitality and long life, were celebrated for their remarkable beauty. It is remarked that on seeing some British youths exposed for sale in the slave markets of Rome and on being told that they were Angles, Gregory exclaimed, "These should not be called Angles but Angels."

There is nothing in these mild climes tending to the production of those evil, distorting passions, alike destructive to manly beauty, health or life. Man here leads a serene and calm existence with neither fear or watchful suspicion of his fellow man, and both mind and body naturally develop to their best perfection.

ANOINTING.

The savage in glossy coat of grease, relieved now and then with a few artistic stripes of high lights, may be an object of merriment to civilized man, but his grease neither chills him nor runs him into a perspiration, it acts as a moderator of either heat or cold, and let the weather become ever so notional, his equilibrium of temper or physiological action goes on undisturbed, his kidneys and liver go on in an unruffled manner and his bowels neither become abnormally relaxed or distressingly apathetic; he finds no fault with the weather and for many of the savages like unto the Sandwich Islander, the word weather is not in their vocabulary. He does not rail at Providence at every change of the weather, or look up at a leaden sky and become dyspeptic. The equability that is maintained by his coat of grease is effective even in the most variable climates. He is as insensible to climatic change as if he lived in the most equable climate in the world; like a sensible fellow, out of a coat of grease he has manufactured for himself an equable climate. This anointing is not alone a practice peculiar to savages, it is as old as Biblical history. Day relates from the classics that on one occasion the Emperor Augustus asked a hale and hearty centenarian by what means he attained such a great an age, " *Intra mulso, foris olio,*" was the answer. The late Dr. Holland remarked that anointing deserved more notice than it had received in the profession, that it was worthy of more extended trial and he was a firm believer in the efficacy of warm oil applied *ad libitum.* I have for years followed the practice of anointing, I grease a new-born babe and the teething child, I have greased scarlet fever and small-pox patients, the dyspeptic, rheumatic and neuralgic; I have them oiled when they are young and when they are old and have every reason to believe that in anointing we have one of the most efficient means, not only as a therapeutic agent or application but also as a means of prolonging life. This oiling is indispensable in variable regions, and I even find it of great benefit in the equable temperature of California when used among the debilitated, either young or old, and now that vaseline offers an oil that does not become rancid or in any way offensive, the practice cannot offer anything objectionable. In ordering the Turkish bath, I always instruct that the person should be thoroughly anointed after the bath has been taken. The ancient habit of the Greeks and Romans of general bathing and anointing could well be revived to the benefit of health and longevity of the modern civilized nations. Oiling takes the place of an equable and constant condition of the atmosphere where it cannot otherwise be obtained, it relieves pain and sensitiveness, promotes a healthy action of the viscera and skin and it lessens the chances for disease. Longevity has no better friend than a good generous coat of olive oil or of vaseline.

DRESS IN SOUTHERN CALIFORNIA.

In the southern part of California, the peculiarly equable climate influences the choice and manner of dress and is most conducive to health and longevity. It never has known extremes of temperature that require either extremes of clothing. It is always too cool for linen and summer clothes, and never cold enough for heavy underwear and heavy winter clothing. Flannel is necessary and agreeable for every day in the year alike; the same heft, texture and color of outer garments is worn for the whole year around; one is not obliged here to wear clothes of one color at one time, and lighter colored at another, to retain or repel the heat of the solar rays; the sun of summer is here not a torrid sun, nor has it that scorching heat that is experienced in the Middle or Western States, but in the language of Thomson:

" The sun has lost his rage, his downward orb
" Shoots nothing now but animating warmth and vital lustre."
—*Thomson's Seasons.*

The same loose comfortable shoes or boots and light felt or even straw head gear can be worn during the whole year, no shrinking wet boots to strain one in drawing them on or off, or wet feet to bring life into risk. He is not obliged to wear any constricting garments or to be weighted down with unusual clothing, he can here dress with the freedom of the Arab. By these means not only does the Southern Californian escape the dangers from variability of weather, and of sudden changes, but he also escapes all dangers incident to not being properly clothed, or that arising from any inconsiderate or untimely change of clothing. Considering the ever present evenness of temperature, the phenomenally aseptic condition of the atmosphere, the natural sobriety in the matter of food and drink, the absence from all dangers that arise from the change of diet or clothing incident to the occurrence of the seasons, constant temptation to out of door exercise, and that the body is never overheated or chilled, and to that absence of that mental worry as to being able to provide against the rigors and sufferings of winter; it is not astonishing that the people of Southern California should enjoy an exceptional and phenomenal immunity from all the diseases of the chest and of the abdominal organs, and contentedly live to a green old age in possession of all their faculties. That dread gauntlet of diseases, that man elsewhere has to encounter at all seasons, appears to us Californians, as fabled as the existence of the maiden-fed monster of Crete, or as mythical as the vicious power of the Grecian Furies.

A recent writer, M. DeSolaville, observes that the greatest number of persons over sixty years of age, is to be found in France, but that that country does not have the greatest number of centenarians. In relation to the longevity of the nations, he notices as follows: " Calculating upon the given age at death we have found a percentage of those among the deceased who are ninety years old and more to be, in Great Britain, 9.73; in Sweden, 7.39; in France, 6.58; in Belgium, 6.07; in Switzerland, 6; in Holland, 4.47; in Italy, 3.76; in Bavaria, 3.42; in Prussia, 3.06; in Austria, 2.61. Throughout Europe as a whole, except Russia, Turkey, and a few smaller States, the same authority tells us that between the year 1869 and 1872, that one out of every 62,503 inhabitants lived to beyond the age of one hundred years. In France from 1823 to 1837 the mean annual number of persons dying centenarians was 162, or one for every 217,105 inhabitants, so that we must look to Great Britain and Denmark and Sweden, for the bulk of the longest lived persons. In the *Sanitarian* for July of 1875, Dana looks upon the British and Danes as being the longer lived races. The well known factor in these different national longevities is simply climate. An equable marine climate favors longevity, and a continental, mountainous and variable climate tends to abbreviate human existence. As observed by Hufeland, Germany has many old people, but not as many very old as her more equably climated neighbors. Hufeland's ideal climate that favors longevity, consists in a marine atmosphere, equable temperature, with a cool rather than a warm medium, a warm soil, with the greatest amount of sunshine and possibility for ventilation and exercise.

Seasons in addition to their extrem es of temperature, which are fatal alike to infancy and old age, have their attendant variability, which as a morbific cause is active at all times and affects all ages. During the first two years of life the temperature of July and August is in the east and middle region of our States the bane of infant life. After our second year, the winter months, especially December, seem to be the months of greatest mortality, this being particularly so from the age of two years to twenty. (*Dr. Wells in Transactions of College of Physicians of Philadelphia, Vol. iv., No. 7.*) Quetelet already mentioned gives December, January, February, and March as being the months most unfavorable to the aged, January having the greatest mortality. Patier, from an analysis of the deaths of ten years at Troyes in France, corroborates the statistics of Quetelet. Confining ourselves more particularly to the vital condition of the aged, we find that with them the number of diseases that tak e them off gradually lessens until, if we are allowed to reach a certain age, our chances of being taken off by disease are so far diminished that we are more liable to go by euthanasia or natural death, without the intervention of disease. Canstatt, Rush, Day, Rostan, Charcot, and all writers on the diseases or conditions of the aged are agreed that structural changes in the blood vessels are the principal causes of death in man when past middle life, atheromatous changes in the coats of the arteries, or cardiac valves, or ossific, or calcareous deposits in the same structures with an increased capacity or hypertrophy of the heart, pave the way for apoplectic attacks, paralysis, or gangrene, and it is in inducing these conditions that variable weather or changeable climates produce a great mortality in the aged. As observed by Baglivi, atmospheric changes so constantly produce apoplexy that the disease at times assumes an epidemic form. Hippocrates observes its frequency in winter in his day, and Andral noticed the same seasonal tendency to apoplexy during his time; pneumonia and heart disease are also more active during the winter or cold months. Extreme heat is as dangerous to the aged, which is particularly observable during any heated spell in the east. As an instance, the week ending July 6, 1872, gave 229 more registered deaths than the cholera week ending July 21, 1866, which stands next to that of 1872 for the largest mortality, even the " grippe " week ending January 14, 1890, having some 400 less deaths than the 2nd week of July, 1872. During this week of excessive deaths, the mean relative humidity was seventy-five per cent, and the mean temperature 83.97°. The increase in deaths affected all ages, but more especially the very young and the very old, as out of a total of 1591 deaths there were 1007 that were children under five years of age and 45 persons who had passed their 70th year; on the second of July of the same week, 68 deaths from direct solar heat took place, the victims being mostly in the prime of life. (*New York Medical Record, August, 1872.*) Two causes evidently co-operate to shorten the existence of the aged: first, the conditions that the coats of the arteries gradually assume as a predisposing cause; and secondly, the extreme ranges of temperature as a determining cause. As observed by Hufeland, " the principal point to be obtained by one wishing to reach old age, consists in always endeavoring to soften and lessen the increasing dryness and rigidity of vessels, which at length occasions the stoppage of the whole machine, and to watch over and promote excretion of corrupted particles which in old age is but imperfectly carried on." This is really the whole secret in a nut shell, or how to live long and enjoy a healthy existence; a study of nature's laws will furnish all the means required to attain these ends.

Let us now look at the question in regard to the pathological conditions as induced by climate, and to the effects of these conditions in lengthening or in shortening the human existence. Morselli has well shown the effects of variability in inducing suicidal tendencies; S. Weir Mitchell has shown its action in producing nervous diseases; Dickinson has well and ably shown its effect in producing renal diseases; Chambers, Kidd, and many others have shown its marked effect in inducing conditions favorable to apoplexy, and its very marked results in precipitating the final catastrophe, and the evidence in relation to the action of variability in inducing pulmonary or chest complaints, or as to its effects in increasing the mortality of infancy, or that of old age, are too conclusive to require more than a passive mention of the facts. But as all the above derangements or accidents, that go to form, as it were, the gauntlet that men must run to reach extreme old age,—all more or less spring from a definite point of departure from the normal where physiological functions or conditions are converted into pathological, as has been well demonstrated by Beale, Black, Fothergill and many others, this condition begins in the changed blood state or condition, and the change is next noticed in the structures and tissues of the vessels, it is well to inquire just how climate produces these disturbances in the economy. It is here that the final results of diet, drink, dress, and habits as induced by climate are eventually harvested, and where the sum total of statistical evidence emphasizes the assertion of Montesquieu that " The Empire of Climate is the most powerful of all Empires;" for it here shows its prerogative over human life in its fullest extent.

I have examined into the physical condition of many of the cases of abnormal longevity met with on this coast, and have noted the absence of any of those arterial changes that we may look for in the aged elsewhere. There is not comparatively as great a diminution of the arterial calibre in the smaller vessels, nor is there comparatively as great a compensating hypertrophy of the cardiac walls; nor are those atheromatous changes or calcareous and ossific deposits in the arterial walls found to have taken place, which render them either softer and more liable to aneurismal dilatation or rupture, or more indurated and brittle, all conditions that abridge their functions, and render man more liable to apoplexy, aneurisms, or to these senile gangrenes and passive congestions that take off so many old people elsewhere. The absence of these pathological conditions enables the skin and the excretory organs to uninterruptedly perform their functions which prevents those retroactive evils that arise from a suppression of excretion through their natural channels, these evils when taking place make themselves evident by the change in the structure and tissue of the vessels whenever excretion is interfered with, the retained matter either acting as a toxic agent in the further determination and degeneration of the vessel walls, or by material deposit in adding to the further rigidity and hardness of the same, and in either case hastening decay and death. The absence of all these pathological conditions in this climate is fully corroborated by the absence or exemption from the diseases to which they tend, as the aged of this climate are not subject to apoplexy, paralysis, senile gangrene, or any of those diseases; this not only applies to the aboriginal inhabitants, but to those born here of European blood, and I have remarked the tendency to those diseases to be greatly diminished, and a tendency to an exemption from the above pathological conditions to be induced in those who have come here before middle life,—this comparative observation being sufficiently easy, as a steady stream of Americans and Englishmen has poured into the country by land and sea through the last fifty years, which furnished ample material for investigation, and that even new comers are greatly benefited in these regards by the climate, I have had sufficient evidence in my own practice.

The northern shores of the Mediterranean, by their variability and liability to sudden changes of meteorological conditions, furnish in this respect, by the prevalence of the diseases induced by the above conditions, a marked contrast to the shores of California, where man may not only expect to live out his full term of life, but do so in all the enjoyment of health and with that vigor of body and all the faculties that come of good health.

WHAT IS THE LIMIT OF HUMAN EXISTENCE?

There is a difference between the average duration of human life and that of its possible limits. In answer to the first, Haller would have placed it at eighty years as that of average old age, but as to its possible extent, he firmly believed that there existed no physiological reason why man should not reach two centuries. That man has a probable duration of from eighty to one hundred years, and a possible duration of from one hundred and fifty to two hundred years was an opinion that not only was held by Haller, but was shared by Hufeland, Flourens, Bertholet, Bushner, Karup and many other scientists. When asked the limit of human existence, Haller replied "*Annos definire, erit difficilius.*" Buffon and Flourens reasoned that if the horse, whose average limit of life is twenty-five years, will in instances live to the age of fifty years, that there are no reasons why man, another mammal, should not likewise at times double the age of eighty and live to one hundred and sixty years. Buffon relates the history of a horse that was sold at the age of ten years by the Duke of Saint Simon to the Bishop of Metz, the horse dying in 1774 at the age of fifty as he was being harnessed. Virey mentions by name eleven cases who had passed one hundred and forty years, three persons who passed one hundred and fifty, and three who had lived beyond one hundred and sixty; one of the latter leaving two children, the oldest being one hundred and three years and the youngest child only nine years old. The records of the celebrated census of Vespasian transcribed by Pliny, returned one hundred and twenty-four persons living between the Appenines and the Po who were from one hundred to one hundred and fifty years of age. Bertholet mentions the case of the traveler Delahaye who reached the age of one hundred and twenty. During the Polish campaign of 1807, Francis Narocki then on the pension rolls of the King of Prussia, whose baptismal certificate proved him to be one hundred and seventeen years old, was presented to Napoleon; Narocki was well and had never been sick, he had a good memory, spoke Latin fluently, and wrote a clear and firm hand. The late French savant M. Chevreul, the late M. Renardin and the still living Senior Admiral of the Fleet, Sir Provo William Wallis, who commanded the frigate Shannon at the close of its action with the Chesapeake off the harbor of Boston, are all examples of past centenarianism that carried their mental and physical activity into their second century of existence. Many of the descendants of Henry Jenkins have been noted for their extreme longevity, which offers ample evidence that longevity was inherent in his organism, with a probability that in prior generations some Jenkins may have even exceeded the length of life of the historical Henry, who died at the age of one hundred and fifty-seven in 1670; late deaths in the same family have shown that they nearly all reach close to a hundred years; there is nothing surprising that an individual like Jenkins coming from a family of centenarians, and living in a climate like that of England, should live to one-third longer than some of his relations; under the circumstances, with that inherent vital tenacity, he could live to two centuries and then not do anything unphysiological or impossible. If Narocki in the inhospitable and rigorous climate of the province of Wilna lived to one-third longer than his fellow old men, there is no reason for doubting but that the same could more easily happen in the mild and favorable climate of the British Isles. Some families die before they reach fifty years, others go to sixty; such vital fibre should not be used as a criterion of cases of abnormal longevity, or as a foundation for any skepticism as to their existence. Jenkins at one hundred and fifty bears the same relation to his centenarian stock that a man of ninety would to his stock were sixty years to be the usual limit of the aged of that particular family, as in either case they have only depassed the usual term of existence of their own kin by one-third longer period. Abnormal longevity comes from long lived stock to begin with, and where the climate offers every facility for its inhabitants to become long lived, there also can the utmost limits of human existence be looked for with a certainty. If this is borne in mind it will be seen that the cases of abnormal longevity that will be related further on, have good reasons for their existence, as the bulk of the population is proverbially long lived—a physical trait that is peculiar to all the Indians of Southern California, as even the Indians of the desert attain great ages, ages far greater than those reached by either the Canadian Indians, or those of the plains, or of the upper valleys of the Missouri or Mississippi as tribes or as a whole. Pasqual, the chief of the Yumas, living in the variable climate of the desert, in the river bottom near Fort Yuma, where the range from the day to night is the greatest in the United States, attained a great age, and to the end of his days ruled his tribe like a Spartan.

In the low temperatured and mild climates of the Peruvian and Columbian Andes centenarianism is common, and we there find ample evidence of cases that go one-third further than their fellowmen in the length of their existence; so that taking what is known of longevity, and what I have since seen of it in California, it has fully converted me to the views of Haller and the others who do not look upon the fact of a human being reaching a century and a half as anything so extraordinary, and to believe with Buffon, that there is no man so old but that he can still hope to become much older. Buffon, and after him Flourens, held that the tendency to abnormal longevity resided solely in the constitution, or as Flourens terms it, the intrinsic value of the internal organs; and that climate, diet or habit had nothing to do with it; in this they were wrong, however, as it is now a well known fact that a small infant mortality, healthy and vigorous prime, comfortable old age and exemption from disease go hand in hand, and that such results are essentially the effects of climatic conditions. Nowhere is this better exemplified than on the west coast of Ireland, where, according to the report made several years ago, by Donnelly and Wilde to the British Parliament, the proportion of diseases generally, and of those of the respiratory organs in particular, was all of two-fifths greater on the eastern than on the western coasts; the same results have been pointed out by others in regard to the two Scottish and English coasts. England, Scotland and Ireland enjoy a wonderful superiority in the matter of infantile viability, general health and longevity over the rest of Europe, yet so essentially climatic is the cause of this superiority that the western shores which are the more affected by the gulf stream, which induces the climate of the whole, have this superiority in a more pronounced degree; there the mass of the population that is born, reach manhood and womanhood with but a small percentage of loss, it being in fact the smallest in Europe, and thence proceed on to old age and longevity; the inhabitants of these countries reaching an average term of existence that is not to be met with in any other European country.

On the Pacific Coast of California longevity is common, examples of extreme length of existence being found at many points, from San Francisco down as far as Cape San Lucas; every Indian rancheria in the mountains, foothills or the coast has some specimens. As in the case of Jenkins, longevity is inherent in the tissues of the inhabitants, and that many should reach ages of from one hundred and ten to one hundred and forty years, and should outstrip their relations by one-third or one-half more of the term of life is neither astonishing or surprising. It is in Southern California that Buffon's saying is fully realized: "Old age is only a prejudice, but for our arithmetic we would not know it; animals do not know it, it is only by our arithmetic that we judge otherwise." Man here more nearly approaches the animal in one respect, than is done anywhere else on the globe. "Man perishes at all ages" says Buffon, "while animals seem to pass through the period of life with firm and steady pace." In this climate, man really lives as if he had lost that inheritance of disease, a habit acquired by a long line of ancestry, whose artificial life has so warped its moral and physical stamina that it has engrafted upon the organism that perverted condition called disease. Here in California, man, with a sound organism at birth, and without the intervention of accidents, can well expect with a minimum amount of prudence, to reach old age, as no diseases to cut life short at any period exist here, with a possibility of dying a natural death when aged, without the intervention of any disease, but like the horse of the Bishop of Metz, to quietly lie down and die in harness.

EFFECT OF SOUTHERN CALIFORNIA CLIMATES.

In the southern part of California where the peculiarities of Syrian Palestine are reproduced; where the climate can be said to be one of perpetual spring; where the same blue and cloudless sky is found as at Bagdad or Damascus; and where life can be passed in the shade of the date palm or the broad-leaved banana; where one may wander in orange groves and perpetual gardens of living flowers amidst playing fountains as in an oriental paradise, we find all the factors requisite for a long life in a stage of perfect health to an extreme degree. Nowhere in the United States can a man retire and live the life of a philosopher, undisturbed by care, want or the elements, as in this portion of California. The mildness of its climate reduces the physical wants of man to a minimum, less food is here required and no great outlay for clothing is demanded. All the precepts of the art of longevity can here be carried into active practice.

Strange as it may seem, the native inhabitants of this portion of California, when found by the early missionaries and explorers, were found to be living under such a state of training and customs, as if some of their ancient chiefs had served a long term of discipleship at the feet of Solon and Lycurgus,—so much like that of the ancient Greeks, did their morals and manners resemble. Physically, they were superior to the red men of the middle or upper coast, both in physique and complexion, as well as in intelligence and manliness of countenance. They wore short cloaks of skins and skirts of the same material; ornaments of ivory and shell-work adorned their persons. According to Bancroft, the Historian of the Coast, from whom this is quoted, the early explorers were quite charmed with the personal beauty of both the men and women whom they found on this southerly coast; they were acquainted with architecture, and many of them lived in properly constructed houses; they used boats and canoes, and for arms they had the bow and arrow and the hardwood saber, and as a tribe they were exceedingly warlike. They were monogamous, and when their children arrived at the age of puberty they passed from the control of the parents, becoming the care of the chiefs, who instructed them in the precepts of abstinence, indifference to hardships and privation; thereby teaching them that physical endurance and indifference and contempt for luxury, were the two attributes of manhood; food considered luxurious was denied to them;

and when in their mountain forays, in the cold and snow-covered altitudes during the winter months, they were forbidden to approach the fire to warm themselves. At his initiation as a warrior, he underwent physical trials, that no candidate for knightly degree would care to undergo; they were instructed to love truth, to do good, and to venerate old age. What a contrast to the naked savage cave-dweller of the more northerly coast;—polygamous and parent-killing, untutored to an extreme degree, and with no more moral responsibility or manly intelligence than was possessed by the wild coyote who disputed the possession of the small game with them. Even the warlike Indians of the upper Mississippi or Missouri valleys had not the moral training or philosophical ideas of those Spartan sages of the Pacific Shores. No tribe of the eastern shores are recorded by the early settlers on the Atlantic Coast as possessing the same stages of civilization.

Their aged, and they had many, were the care of the community. Dr. W. A. Winder, of San Diego, tells me, that on a visit to El Cajon Valley, made some thirty years ago, he was taken to the house in which a number of these aged persons were being cared for; there were in the valley some half dozen who had reached an extreme age; some were unable to move, their bony frame being seemingly ankylosed; they were old, wrinkled, and blear eyed; their skin was hanging in leathery folds about their withered limbs; some had hair as white as snow and had seen some seven scores of years; others still able to crawl, but so aged as to be unable to stand, went slowly about on their hands and knees, their limbs were attenuated and withered. The organs of special sense had in many nearly lost all functional activity some generations back, some had lost the use of their limbs for more than a decade or a generation; but the organs of life and the great sympathetic still kept up their automatic functions,—not recognizing the fact and seemingly indifferent that the rest of the body had ceased to be of any use, a generation or more in the past. These thoracic and abdominal organs, and their physiological actions being kept alive and active, as it were against time, and the silent and unconscious functional activity of the great sympathetic and its ganglia, shows a tenacity of the animal tissues to hold on to life that is phenomenal.

A Lewis or a Thoms may ask how do you know these Indians to be as old as represented. It must be borne in mind that these Indians were not migratory, they all lived within certain limits and were well known to each other. The early Missions established by the Franciscan Friars, were built with the assistance of Indian labor. The dates of the construction of these Missions are matters of history and of record, and many of the incidents were not only recorded in their relations, but the Mission Fathers have handed much down that is historical, from Friar to Friar and from Friar to Priest by word of mouth. Besides these, there is a knowledge of the Indians regarding each other, and especially regarding those who have attained to ages that made them venerable and entitled to respect. From all of these, and the carefully kept records of family and personal events, births, marriages and deaths, found in the records of the different Missions, we have sufficient reliable testimony from which to reach the true state of their ages. Father A. D. Ubach has known a number who were employed at the building of the Mission of San Diego, an event which happened nearly a century before he took charge of this Mission, these men had been engaged in carrying timber from the mountains, or in making brick; many of these were still living within the last twenty years. There are still living some Indian women at the Indian Village at Capitan Grande, whose ages he estimates at over one hundred and thirty years.

With the advent of the Mission Fathers and the breaking up of their tribal relations, the power formerly exercised by the chiefs was assumed by the Church, which also replaced the common routine farm labor and herding for the industrial pursuits which were then carried on by the Missions, as well as dependent obedience for their former warlike training and Spartan virtues. And when the Church gave up the charge of its proteges at its secularization, and they began to mingle with American civilization, with its border morality and in its pioneer dissipation, it is needless to say, that the last vestiges of Spartanism and all its benefits were not slow in disappearing. The aged were more or less neglected, and from this neglect many of them died.

Dr. Edward Palmer, long connected with the Agricultural Department and with the Smithsonian Institute, who has spent over twenty years in familiarizing himself with the natural history of this region, and is perfectly conversant with the past and present history and customs of the Indians of Southern and Lower California, in sending me a photograph some time ago said, " This is the aged squaw I told you of, she was one hundred and twenty-six years of age, she is the same one whom I saw put six watermelons in a blanket, tie it up and carry them on her back for two miles." In conversation with the doctor he informed me that having heard of her extreme age, and of her great endurance and capabilities,—so abnormal at her time of life,—he had purposely visited the encampment for the purpose of investigation. He saw her perform the feat of carrying the watermelons for the distance of two miles for the purpose of marketing them; he was very much astonished to find that she never stopped even for rest; he had no doubt as to her age, she was perfectly conversant with the tribal habits which she had seen practiced, such as cremation of the dead, which the Mission Fathers had compelled them to relinquish. In conversation she was bright and her memory good; she detailed to Dr. Palmer incidents of flogging by the Fathers, to which they had subjected the Indians as a punishment, for still indulging themselves in the cremation of their relations; from this and other incidents which she related, the doctor was well satisfied that she must have existed at the time of their occurrence. From his own knowledge of Indian history and their customs, and the time of the changes that were made in their modes of living and in their habits, and by a careful cross-examination into the different subjects and their details, he satisfied himself that her information was not obtained from hearsay or tradition.

Down on the coast of Lower California, some distance below San Diego, near the old Mission of San Tomas, there is still living an old Indian, bent and wrinkled, whose age is computed at one hundred and forty years; although blind and going naked, he is still active, and daily goes down to the beach and along the beds of the creeks in search of drift wood, making it his daily task to gather and carry to the encampment a faggot of wood.

Philip Crosthwaite, who has lived here since 1843, has an old man on his ranch, who mounts his horse and rides about daily, who was a grown man breaking horses for the Mission Fathers when Don Antonio Serrano was an infant. Don Antonio I know quite well, having attended him through a serious illness some sixteen years ago. Although now at the advanced age of ninety-three, he is erect as a pine, and he rides his horse with his usual ease and grace; he is thin and spare, but very tall, and those who knew him fifty years ago or more remember him as the most skillful horseman in the neighborhood of San Diego. And yet as fabulous as it may seem, the man who danced this Don Antonio on his knee when an infant, is not only still alive, but active enough to mount his horse and canter about the country. This may sound Rider Haggardish, but it is neverthe-less a fact. Some years ago I attended an elderly gentleman, since dead, who knew this old man as a full grown man, when he and Don Serrano were play-children together. From a con-versation with Father Ubach, I learned that the man's age is perfectly authenticated to be beyond one hundred and eighteen years.

Out on the Sweetwater, there lives an old Indian of the age of one hundred and fifteen. Dr. Robert J. Gregg has carefully in-vestigated his history, and both he and Father Ubach are per-fectly satisfied as to that being his age. Dr. Gregg tells me that he is one of the first Indians he has·met with a keen sense of humor and the ridiculous. The old man thoroughly enjoys a joke and is a great talker, he is wonderfully active and a great walker, and always on the go,—a fifty mile trip, going and returning from the mountains for a bag of acorns which he packs on his back, is a matter of no moment for the old gentle-man;—he lives frugally and always has been exceedingly ab-stemious and temperate. When he walks into town, a distance of twenty-five miles from his home, he carries an old pair of pants carefully rolled up under his arm, to put them on on the outskirts of the city. He generally goes with nothing on but a shirt and a small loose perineal band. As he remarked in a jocu-lar way to the doctor, "I went too long without breeches, they make my legs perspire, which I don't like; but as I have been told that the ladies of San Diego don't admire bare legs, espe-cially mine which are somewhat old and wrinkled, so that I put up with the discomfort of the breeches, and the consequent perspiration while about town out of deference to their feelings, but I take them off as soon as I get in the suburbs of town on my return." The old man speaks his native Indian and Span-ish, which he learned when a young man, and he is full of in-formation relating to the early history of the Mission.

There was an old man living in the eastern part of San Diego

City, whom I visited when sick at the age of one hundred and nine, the man belonged to the Mission Indians and had always lived in the foot hills and the coast adjacent to San Diego. He recovered from his illness and did not die until the year afterwards. In the intervening time, between the illness of a year ago and that of his death, he had enjoyed perfect health; even when at that advanced age, he daily walked several miles without any extra exertion and carried burdens and made himself generally useful. His wife who still survives him is also a very old person, and has been blind for over thirty years. It was affecting to watch the affection that existed between these two old persons. The old man never touched a morsel of food that was given to him, no matter how little or how much, until he had first taken it to his wife, and given her the choicest pieces; when together they looked to each other's comforts, and at the time he was sick, no sister of charity could have shown more attention or consideration than this poor old blind woman did to her sick husband. Mr. Joseph Manasse and Father Ubach, who have had this old couple under their care for many years, and others who have known them for a few generations or more, have given me sufficient proof that his age was one hundred and ten at his death! Dr. Edward Palmer, already referred to, has also kindly sent me the particulars of an old man named Justiniano Roxas of Santa Cruz, who died in 1875 at the age of one hundred and twenty-three. Roxas was the name given him at baptism, he was an Indian of the Santa Cruz tribe, and as Dr. Palmer informed me, never would adopt the Spanish diet and mode of eating as to quantity or quality, but throughout his long years, he persisted in his simple original habits of diet and abstemiousness and to the last, like the old man of the Sweetwater above-mentioned, maintained his habits of steady exercise. From Father Ubach, who is thoroughly conversant with the personal habits of all these old persons, I learned that in every instance their habits had been those of strict temperance and abstemiousness, and he attributes their very long lives to the extreme simplicity of their diet, which in the many cases of extreme age, that he is conversant with, has consisted simply of acorns, flour and water. There is something grand about these old men and so inconsistent with our ideas of the ordinary Indian; that they should have adhered throughout all these years to their simple modes of life when surrounded, as they were, by temptations that a savage can hardly withstand. If we admire a Diogenes or a Socrates, who had everything in their favor and the advantages of education, to say nothing of the gratification of a certain kind of vanity,—how much more are these poor, simple and untutored savages, who followed the same path of virtue, entitled to our admiration, especially as it was done from a sense of duty to self, without any vanity to gratify or expectation of applause.

The reader may think that the estimate of the climate, as a factor of longevity, has been over estimated. Some reflections will satisfy the most skeptical, that this estimate has not been overdrawn.

It is but necessary to look at the causes of death and at their frequency, and the ages that they are most likely to attack, to understand that the less of these causes that are present, the greater are the chances for man to reach longevity. Add to these reflections, that you here run no gauntlet of diseases to undermine or deteriorate the organism, that in this climate childhood finds an escape from those diseases which are the terror of mothers and against which physicians are helpless, as we have here none of those affections of the first three years of life, so prevalent during the summer months in the East and the rest of the United States, then again the absence of gastric and intestinal diseases is almost incredible. This immunity extends through every age of life. Hepatic and kindred disorders are also unknown. Of lung affections, there is no land that can boast of a like exemption. Be it the equability of temperature or the aseptic condition of the atmosphere; the free sweep of winds or absence of disease germs, or what else it may be ascribed to, but one thing is certain, there is no pneumonia, bronchitis or pleurisy lying in wait for either the infant or the aged.

The great deteriorator and poisoner of the human tissues, and prime factor of so much premature decay in the body, malaria, is here conspicuous only by its absence. Renal diseases are remarkable from their rarity, there is nothing either in the climate or in the water that is drank, that will produce calculus or any kindred disorders. The equability of the temperature and the sobriety encouraged by the climate both as to food and drink, tends to prevent any of those irregularities of kidney action, and blood changes, so productive of kidney structural change in variable regions. Rheumatism, which, as a climatic product, is so prevalent in Japan that imported horses, even, soon become its victims, is in this climate so rare that ringbone and bone-spavin, those products of chronic or acute rheumatism in the horse, are here unknown, although the native Californian horse has known neither stabling, shelter or care. In the temperate and equable climate of the coast and foot-hills the Indians likewise know no rheumatism, which, however, is no stranger to the Indian in the extremely variable atmosphere of the desert. A like immunity is also enjoyed from skin diseases. Sunstroke and hydrophobia are likewise foreign to this climate. In fact all of the diseases of the variable Northern part of the Temperate Zone, as well as the more dreaded affections of the South and of the Tropics are here unknown, and there exists an utter absence of anything like endemic diseases. It results, therefore, that from childhood to old age there are no deteriorating influences to encounter, and green old age is reached, with an organism unimpaired and fully able to perform all its physiological functions, which enables the body to prolong its physical existence to that extreme limit, that makes euthanastic death in this climate, not only a possibility but a probability.

CONCLUSIONS.

Southern California possesses every requisite for the prolongation of human life. Hufeland's idea of climate is here realized. In his day, the nearest approach to perfection were the insular regions to the north of Great Britain, where latitude, sea-level and the genial warmth of the gulf stream concerted to its production. In those islands, however, the equability, the warmth of the soil and the almost constant sunshine of Southern California were wanting. The second of these factors, a warm soil, is mentioned by Hufeland as highly favorable and necessary to the prolongation of human life, it being a more important factor than is generally mentioned. The dangers arising from cold and the susceptibility of the aged to cold have already been referred to. The experimental but successful practices of the early disciples of homeopathy in the case of King David, and the later use of physical warmth by Bœrhaave with the frigid Dutch burgomaster, to prolong life, are but evidences that the recognition of gentle warmth as an element necessary to the preservation of life is a matter of long standing. A damp cold soil, and a dry warm soil such as that of Southern California, have entirely opposite effects on the vitality of the body; the first dwarfs its forces and abbreviates the length of life, whilst the second condition strengthens and prolongs its days. This subject of soil warmth, its causes and conditions, is an interesting part of California climatology, the object and length of this paper will, however, only allow a mention of its effects, with the incidental remark, that from the observations of the writer, which extend to the soils of the Coast of Southern France, Italy and Spain, that none can approach that of Southern California for its constancy in this regard.

Another element greatly favoring longevity is the absence of seasons and the consequent dangers incurred by not properly adjusting the diet to seasonable requirements. Brackenridge maintained that in Great Britain, consumption originated during the summer season owing to the great lack of fats, which at that season do not enter sufficiently into the dietary tables of the homes, and that on the approach of the winter the disease is developed; his arguments are very ingenious and plausible. There is no doubt that in the Temperate Zone, at least in the northern portions of it, if the diet of winter should be carried too far into the spring months serious injury would result, as well as that the meager and spare diet of the summer but ill prepares the body for that resistance that is required during the winter. In variable regions where changes are abrupt and where sometimes one season is unceremoniously ushered in before the other is quite done, it naturally follows that health, and consequently the duration of life, must necessarily suffer materially; especially the old who are feeble and are not calculated to resist such sudden changes.

Infancy, invalid middle age, and old age are all alike sensitive to sudden changes or great variations of temperature or to any deteriorating influences. In a paper read before the Medical Society of the District of Southern California in 1889, and published in the transactions of that meeting, the writer showed by the mortality reports gathered for a number of consecutive years from different European nations, representing the mild as well as the extreme variable types of climate, that however vigorous the adult population of mountain regions may be in their prime, that the infant mortality is there exceedingly excessive, whereas the most equable climate gives the less mortality. Wherever infants do well and have the greatest chances of life, there old age will also be sure to flourish. Marine climates favor both infancy and old age, the statistics of the British Registrar General are very conclusive on this point. Unprofessional men often wonder how men can live and be healthy without the stimulus of seasonal change, seeming to think that a periodical revolution is in some indescribable way a necessity to health, and that in the absence of this revolutionary action or stimulus affecting the system, that the body must necessarily suffer. A careful perusal of Richardson, and of the tables of Buchan and Mitchell, and of the experiments of Mr. Milner, Medical Superintendent of the Wakefield Convict Establishment, or of the works of S. Wier Mitchell, and of Bennett, Bell and others, will at once convince them of the dangers of seasonal change to the human economy. Larrey in his Surgical Memoirs and Morselli in his admirable work on Suicide also furnish any amount of evidence detailing the destructive influence of seasonal change on the human constitution, and of its deteriorating influence on longevity. Winter diseases do not occur in summer, nor do those of summer in the winter; then there are the diseases peculiar to spring and those of the fall, which certainly do not exist where such seasons are not to be found, and the diseases peculiar and incident to the periods when one season is changing into the other, or to those derangements brought about by the sudden infusion of a few days of weather characteristic of one season into the middle of the opposite season, which are escaped where these changes are not to be found. Disease waves follow certain meteorological conditions which seem to create them, and sudden changes or great variability seem to increase their dangerous character, the variability and changes being more dangerous than either extreme. As demonstrated by Larrey, during the Russian campaign, or when the French army was in the mountains of Spain, man can stand a great degree of cold even when freely exposed to it, providing that the conditions remain constant, and it was also demonstrated that even a change to greater cold than the one experienced at the moment, is harmless, but that a change to warmth may be very disastrous. The Baron informs us that so well are these facts understood in Poland and in Russia, that the inhabitants of those countries would not think of undertaking a long and serious journey during the winter season, until assured that the period of settled and constant cold had arrived.

Man can stand a great amount of exertion in either extreme of temperature. The laborers in the New Liverpool Salt Works, in the great depression below sea-level in the great Colorado Desert, labor and endure the great heat of that region with seeming indifference, and with less discomfort and exhaustion than a farm laborer would experience in any of the harvest fields of the Mississippi Valley. Lieutenant Schwatka, the Arctic explorer, informed the writer that on one occasion he had walked eighty-two miles in twenty-four hours during extreme Arctic weather, and in a constant very low temperature. Any one who knows the Lieutenant can readily understand that with his physique and muscular strength and great power of endurance, especially when nerved up as he was in this instance, the object of the trip being to send back food and assistance to his Esquimaux escort who had given out, that such a trip was for him under the circumstances an easy possibility. This is also another example of the superior pluck and endurance of man born in a mild climate when compared with those born in a rigorous climate, with the trial taking place under their own skies. On the same rations of food and subjected to the same trials the Esquimaux had completely given out, and but for the nerve and superior vitality, vigor and endurance of the Lieutenant they would all have perished.

The Southern California Coast possesses no seasons, and, therefore, no seasonal changes, but a climate of a constant uniformity, which is necessarily exempt from the whole category of diseases, ailments or derangements that arise from or are aggravated by those causes. This explains the phenomenal immunity that this region enjoys from pulmonary or abdominal diseases of all classes as well as how it is the elysium of longevity.